LOVE SONGS

Prayers to Gods, Not Men

Olga Stein

AOS Publishing, 2025
ISBN: 978-1-998662-26-5

Cover image: *Goddess*
by Maxime Stein

Visit AOS Publishing's website:
www.aospublishing.com

For Jacob, Maxime, and Simone

Table of Contents

Author's Note

Love Songs: Prayers to Gods, Not Men is a collection of poems that examines love from a variety of artistic, intellectual, and cultural vantage points. Love shows up as different facets of Eros: expressions of passion or desire that speak through various registers of emotion and compel the poet to write; and philosophical constructs, such as Plato's notion of Eros as a tempering force that elevates lovers and humankind on the whole. Other shades of Eros are depicted as selfless, nurturing, or compassionate love, resembling *philia* and *agape*. These poems look at relationships between lovers, parents and children, and between mortals and the gods they turn to for artistic inspiration and guidance, support, or vengeance.

Philosophers and poets have posed the question— what is love?—since time immemorial. Alt1hough universally acknowledged as a transformative force, love retains much of its original mystery and mythos. Here, I've drawn answers from the high and low of art and experience, and interpolated women's voices as a way of challenging standard authority/ies on the subject. Moreover, poetry and poets themselves, our modern-day minstrels, become objects of scrutiny in a number of the poems. In a turning of the tables on the archetypal seductress, male poets become the sirens whom women should fear. Needless to say, the female author is quick to acknowledge (with a knowing wink) her own complicity in a creative practice that surreptitiously disarms readers.

This collection makes certain demands of readers. There are numerous intertextual allusions to gods, Homer, Plato, Ovid, Horace, Virgil, and a number of iconic characters in Classical narratives. Readers should be prepared to acquaint themselves with ancient myths and the figures that remain with us in works of literature, visual art, and music. Similarly, tropes many of us have come to associate with the writings of ancient philosophers and poets are put to use here to refigure love and romantic entanglements—that is, ideal partners, and those to be wary of, love as a gift or as a force we cannot control or predict.

Allusions to poets, ancient and modern, broaden the cultural context and provoke friction between competing notions of love. In the same vein, I've deployed popular culture and musical terms in this collection to give spin or effect an estrangement from common meanings and assumptions. Readers will find themselves contemplating a number of juxtapositions and appositions; these poems talk with each other and sometimes against one another.

Almost all of the poems wrestle with love and sexuality. Both are framed variously as benisons to be celebrated, as impulses and proclivities to be controlled and repressed, or as natural human tendencies that are essential for survival and creativity, but that call for wisdom and discipline. The author hopes readers will find a dialogue on love—agreement and disagreement on what love can or should offer. Ultimately, the collection functions as a meta-poetic commentary on the writing of poetry (as well as its reception), and the poet's own efforts to express herself through this art form.

This collection has two sections, "gods" and "Tales." The first section, "gods," directly addresses gods, spirits, and their proxies (not always benevolent) in shorter poems; the second section, "Tales," features longer, narrative poems intertextually linked to a larger historical canvas of works on love. The final and longest poem in this collection, "Excavating Torment (Or Ekphrastic Intertextuality)," demonstrates how ekphrasis and intertextuality work in poetry, painting, and sculpture, while tracing the use of these creative elements back to the fourth century BCE.

Will readers find themselves or their experiences reflected in these poems? Highly likely—whenever the poet speaks in the guise of spurned lover or an older and wiser one, whether as a parent, partner, or an independent-minded woman who defines love (and poetry) for herself. Most especially, these poems will resonate with readers in possession of a wide range of literary and conceptual references, who enjoy the intertextual play between ideas and their reifications in poetry.

Finally, the Notes pages and Bibliography at the back of the collection are intended to serve readers who are curious about the meanings of certain terms, or would like to track instances of intertextuality to their original sources.

gods

Eros

Eros, munificent spirit or godhead,
Let your turbulence keep me aloft for a spell.
Let me be carried on unrepressed ardor
And let my pen venture, indifferent to censure.
Eros, you've been either praised or reviled
Since Helen's amour was decried as obscene
By those dreading excess—theologians, logicians,
Also some Platonist metaphysicians.

Angels and demons aren't folklore and myth.
Freud labelled them signs of unfulfilled yearnings.
Stories of gods, wanton or wrathful,
Recreate our frustrations and deep-seated longings—
Discontents that puncture civilization's veneers,
Rattle the shackles of psychic wraiths
Who pattern and shape subliminal fears.

Puckish Eros, my friend, help me fly without scruple,
Oblivious of divisions betwixt the sacred and profane.
Let others decide; the distinction is subtle, and
I've always found them to be one and the same.
Eros, quickening, lightening-strike passion,
Let me mount you and ride through blistering fire,
Harness the power that'll compel me to fashion
Stanzas that scorch with unbridled desire.
Priests speak of Eros as ungovernable emotions,

Which arise from below the transverse plane.
A line that separates body and spirit,
The noble and base; the sane and insane.
Our inferior parts—not the ego, but id—
Are humanity's bane, Freud famously claimed.
Though blame shifts to Eros when mayhem prevails,
The root cause of grief isn't rapture but creed.

Amor begets madness, most will object.
It dazes, shakes, then emboldens its subject
To do, say, or write words that others abjure.
Yet you reward those eschewing a cure.
Like Sappho, those resolved not to spurn you will ride
Over sky-piercing summits, across surging oceans,
Toward the sun's searing brightness, and on—
without fear
To gaze on aeonian motions of celestial spheres.

Uncommon texts tap transcendent emotions
Of terror and awe, and love unrestrained.
Sublime depictions are true evocations
Of spirits immortal and forces untamed.
Eros, my wild one, let the world spin past;
Let me mount you and ride
Without saddle or rein.
Only let me hold fast to your rough heady mane.

The Ladder

My window looks on to a ladder,
which leans against the parapet
belonging to the house next door.
During the day, the buffed surface
of the concrete wall serves as a stage
for dream-inducing, buoyant shadows,
aqueous distortions of leafy branches,
birds, cars, and passersby.
Quivering, spectral, these visions
seem to transpose reality, like an egress
to some beyond—a realm
that parallels the world I'm in,
where I, a consciousness adrift,
sit staring out the window.
Meanwhile, even the ladder
shivers in the sun, deliquesces,
and from the topmost metal rung,
a steady gleam compels my gaze to climb.
The rooftop, now a hazy promontory,
holds out the promise of a limpid view,
an epiphanic glimpse, were I to ascend
the ladder and, standing in the light,
survey the slate-blue world below.
I meditate on the prospect of an ascent,
picture myself perched vertiginously
on a ledge, an overhang. I am on the verge
of being summoned from on high

by some austere, haughty god.
The vision shimmers hypnotically,
scatters my thoughts, though not for long.
Soon I recover, adjust, revise.
The deck I stand on I now imagine
as an Aegean water's edge,
from where I gaze at a cerulean sea.
The ladder, half-submerged, tempts me
with the promise of immersion,
in cool, undulating splendour,
where I can float in soundless reverie.
Beneath me are fathoms of sibylline blue,
a vast ether, which I intuit as the purview
of a potent god. I sense her generative presence
in the pulsating depths, and offer her thanks
                              out of gratitude and dread.

Your Subject

Your poem is about love,
About another woman.
She remains on the page,
Though not in your life.
Now I am
Launched into your text, displacing her.
Physics teaches us displacement.
Is a body replacing another body,
Making the vessel full again.
Will I do
Long enough to become a poem?
A page or two in a book?
Will I make a final edition?
Or will I be displaced
By shapelier lines or
A more book-worthy body?

The Poet

Beastly poet, treacherous beast.
You lured me into the jungle
just for the hunt of it,
flayed me and left
me there, on the ground, bleeding everywhere,
face in the torturous growth of your indifference
and my misplaced trust.
Women know the score.
We've been forewarned—"The Poet"—remember?
My fault, then, for not seeing through your lines,
for not turning a deaf ear to your false come-ons,
for letting you take me by the hand
and drag me to hell.
But so you know,
in the end, I healed.
I got on my feet,
I dusted you off.
And I want to say this:
Day or night,
I was always the better poet.

Love and Death in the Multiverse

Quantum physics posits multiple worlds
lines them up, per theory,
so they unfold in parallel
without touching. Everettian enthusiast
holds court, enraptured, smiles,
blethers on volubly apropos the premise:
multiverse, its scores of worlds,
with variations on us in each.
Intriguing, sure. I nod, doubtful.
Still, I'm willing to muse—not on the math,
but over what's real or unreal.

Yesterday, or possibly last week,
I saw a photo of the NGC 6302.
Its dying star formed two wings,
accretions of a giant nebula,
composed of multicoloured clusters.
Beauteous in its pelerine of stellar gas and dust,
this celestial marvel looked to me
like two universes converging in a kiss.

Le bisou, I think, glancing sideways,
try to picture us in alternate universes:
Short-lived flickers in infinite time;
perhaps, parts in a story staged over and over.

If we die here, do we die elsewhere?
It might be fair to say our endings are synched.
Then again, it could work like chain reactions,
inducing slow implosions. Terminal illness?
That would make cancer the antimatter.

I wonder, *What happens when we love in one world?*
Do the powers of attraction hold
between two particles in every universe?
Or are we drawn together by chance
here only, not multiversally?
Then wouldn't we be stray elements
whose valencies are varied,
and whose fusion would depend fully
on the vagaries of fate?

Photograph

That picture of him in Moscow
Standing against the Kremlin:
His six-foot-six frame,
Seemingly ageless, robust,
A storied Grecian, posing relaxed.
The vivid background barely competes;
His toothy smile, captivating,
Is the natural focal point.

I'm spellbound by the form.
Can't tell which is the more splendid,
Which the more glorious architecture.
It's not the beguiling features,
The classically-perfect proportions,
But the height that never fails to amaze.
His length and lineaments thrill me.

Likewise, the contours of his face.
When we were close
I delighted in its genealogical markings,
Discerning traces of older civilizations—
Moorish, Spanish, Native Latin American—
In his forehead, eyes, and cheekbones.

I loved the accent of his speech,
The language that gave rise to it,
The lips from which he uttered,

The words that gave me joy.
I cherished all of him.

Now that it is over, I wonder
At the largesse of my heart,
Its imprudent, unreserved capacity
To love, accommodate, and
Overlook so much.
It is a marvel how the heart enfolds
The full breadth of a man,
His limitations.

Rejection

You discarded me
Right after your taste test,
Like I was a thing that looked good,
But wasn't when in your mouth.
After all those ooohs and aaahs,
Announcing your e-mails,
Verbal foreplay that worked on me,
Though I thought it corny at first.
At first, I had no eyes for you,
Your scarred face
Well-defined, I admit, delicate—
Too delicate for my delectation, I thought.
But your manner charmed me,
Something fine about your hands,
A refinement to which I'm partial—your form.
How easily you hooked me!
I controlled the situation at first,
Power was all mine, I thought,
Your interest being stronger.
But the body has its own volition.
The balance shifted despite
The absence of capital letters in your emails
(I like the maleness of declared starts
And closures—so sue me).
I never fell for your writing,
Only you, the sweet idea of you,
A story I told myself,
Whose ending makes me sad.

Riffing on Neruda

Neruda (Sonnet XLIV in italics):

You will know that I don't love you and that I love you
given that life is made of two ways,
the word is one wing of silence,
half of fire is cold.

Never will you know the fullness of my love.
I keep it half-hidden, half-masked.
Feigning and dissembling, fooling even myself
into a coldness that burns because it is a lie.

I love you in order to begin loving you,
to start infinity again
and never to stop loving you:
that is why I do not love you yet.

I cannot recall the time before I loved you.
It happens in an infinitely distant past.
And yet I seek to recreate that time, that instant when
my love burst into existence like a small universe.

I love you and do not love you as if I had
in my hands the key of joy
and a wretched uncertain fate.

The once-possible is possible no longer:
Impossible not to equate you with joy,
and impossible to believe that such joy can be had.

Horror

When you left me
It was like you tore off my arm.
The punishment I suffered was barbaric
All because of those brief moments I was cold to you.
My, what a huge ego you have.
The better to stab me with, eh?

So I made you die in my heart;
I shot you (I won't say where),
Then dug you a chasm for a grave,
Filled it with earth,
And stomped on it with unrestrained glee.
But that wasn't enough;
I wound silver chains around you,
Watched your skin blister and burn.
The sound of it sizzling
Soothed my ears.

This didn't do it either;
I tried chains again,
This time around your wrists and ankles.
I lowered you into a glass coffer,
Filled it with water, and watched you writhing
Houdini-like until you drowned.
I was delirious at the sight.
Now you're a blackened corpse,
All of you swollen, begrimed—a fright,

Yet refusing to die.
You keep coming for me,
Accursed blackguard, cease!
Telling me you want me now,
Threatening to suck me dry.
I pray I'll have the strength to resist.

Confessional

"I don't write confessionally," I say, drawing closer.
My animal self wallows in the warmth,
the feel of skin-to-skin.
I breathe his scent, the sweet musk, picture myself a
critter sniffing contentedly
the freshly-dug soil, roots of verdure, and tiny insect
lives blissfully tucked deep inside, unseen.
The large muscles of his back relax. I'm well received.
His quiet pulse blends with my own organic rhythms.
We're like wolves nestled in their den. I'm half-asleep.

"But isn't it par for the course nowadays?"
His question disrupts the cradling stillness,
nudges me back into awareness.

I say, "Professionally speaking, it's not prudent to bare
ourselves for all to see.
It's not just our erotic natures, our untamed cravings that
could bewilder readers.
It's hurt and rage—the subterranean stuff, much of it too
unseemly, it seems to me,
for poetry to purify." I tap him. "Do you agree?"

Truth is, I'm hesitant to translate into poetry
the darker matter
of my compulsions, a tendency to scratch old wounds,
the surfeit of guilt and dread plaguing my dreams—
especially the latter.

All this I deplore in myself, and more
that I'm afraid to air.
Some nights, it's as if I'm being devoured from within
by a vampiric fiend. A paralyzing sense of dissolution
creeps in.
I gasp, staring into the dark, feeling like I'm barely there.

Besides, I've always been ambivalent about the *con* in
fessing up, distrusting performance in poetry,
the kind strutting its truth.
Are there *beaux mots* for anguish?
How much is straight up, heads-up personal?
For most of us, what's real is indelicate, uncouth.

"Too much confessing ends in a morass," I tell him,
then wonder about redemption.
Do metaphors ensure ascension,
help flowers grow in muck?
Plath was remorseless. She reified her angst
in striking, fertile tropes, whereas
I fear the gawking and mockery of the ruck.

Silently, I weigh my reasons, thinking:
it's best to keep the curtains down on my proclivities,
my sins.
Stretching an arm, I run my nails against the skin
of his shoulder, then dig in.

Soul Mate

We made love in hotel rooms
Where the halls had ears.
We repressed nothing.
Ah, the irreverence of it.

Our lovemaking, primal, wild,
Transgressed all decorum.
We let each other loose on the bed
To the rhythms of natural lust.

You were the first to bring me face-to-face
With the lawlessness of my desire.
Your words alone made me combustible—
Ah, the wonder of your beguiling words.

My singer of psalms,
I soared within your sweet embrace.
I rose on ecstasy, past myself
On the transcending force of it.

When I look at my daughters now,
I wonder whether they'll find a David of their own
To anoint them with all the ways of love.
Ah, to find the complement to one's soul.

Prayers to gods

I. Horoscope
August 28, 2024

Your dreams
may feel more real
than whatever
appears solid
before you.

Have confidence —
Venus pays heed to your desires.
Let your visions
transport you anywhere
at will.
Any port of call will do.

Set aside extraneous tasks.
Return to them
under more munificent skies.

II. Horoscope
September 5, 2024

A profound soul connection
could materialize on your horizon!

Thanks to beautiful Venus' drift
toward relationship-bound Libra,
the shored up gravity
could attract
a long-sought suitor.

Journeys

Picture men boarding
sea-worthy vessels,
whispering prayers to gods or
demi-deities:
Let us stay on course,
help us withstand the ocean's
mysteries, its unfathomable
force.
They pitch these entreaties
at hallowed ears
only half-bent to mortal men,
and women, left ashore to
wait with gnawing fear,
wait and supplicate,
daily scanning the horizon,
worry beads in hand.

A distraught liaison
will barter her own life
for *him* to make land.

Searching

Aristophanes expounds on
humankind and Love.
Love is the fulfilment of
yearning for
our other half,
our soul partner.
He says, *At first, the human*
animal had four legs,
four arms,

Celtic wisdom conjures an
 'Anam Cara,' meaning
'soul friend.' They wait for us.

If we're fortunate
and find them —
with help from the stars —
we experience a bond
that transcends all others.

was male and female.
Then gods demanded it be
punished for arrogance,
so Jupiter split
the upstart creature in two.
Since then, Aristophanes
implies, we go about
disconsolate, feeling
the absence of our other self,
searching. If we find them,
we gain love that completes
us like no other.

III. Horoscope

September 14, 2024
Look for recurring symbols
Is there water imagery?
Aquatic scenes indicate
depth, complexity,
the need to trust your heart.

Patterns have meanings
that merit our attention.
No one is destined
to fail or succeed
in Love, or other ventures.

For instance, the sun gives hope
but has its doleful side.
The sun can scorch,
desiccate living things.
Mars, too, can portend
opportunities or hurdles.

Star Taking

You're on the deck of a ship.
An endless, undulating blue
surrounds you.
No object to discern—
blankness, not a blip
on the horizon to help decode
the oceanic vastness.
No squall, kraken, or siren
    (*thank the gods*)!
Yet overhead, neither a gull
    nor albatross—
Ask, then, *What are your*
odds? Weeks without signs
by which to steer,
'cept the sun, moon,
constellations, floating in
the celestial sphere.
A mariner's astrolabe,
Ptolemy's calculations

Each object calls for
nuanced readings;
each bequeathes
precious guidance.

to read stars, measure
latitudes, reveal locations.
At sea, astronomy will
restore a sailor to his love
if glowing *aeiphanes* and
Virgo assist with navigation
from above.

Understand what matters
most to you.
Then make it a reality.

Begin with a blank page,
    let an idea guide you,
    or ancient lore,
    or metaphor.

Revenge

Ladies, beware!
Sentences are weapons
For those skilled in lobbying pretty ones
Like delayed grenades,
Or flames readily fanned.
They spray us with words
That vaporize our precious self-possession.
It's time to thwart and disarm
Cocksure scribblers—writers and poets—
Those who turn words into stealth weapons,
Stun us with phrases and similes.
Watch out! They sound melodies like sirens,
Ruthlessly charm us into senselessness
So they can strike unimpeded.

What motivates such cruel attacks,
Fruitless forays into our trusting hearts?
Let me tell you—
They blast their way in, devastate,
Then leave professing innocence,
Intimating we had wantonly opened the gates
Ourselves, inviting the onslaught.
Why do they do it?
Because they can!

Time now to neutralize their weapons,
Take apart their missile-like missives,

Leave no word unturned, unprobed
For freshness and verve,
Syntactical care and plain good sense.
Men who write have delicate egos,
Armor that's easily punctured
With tactically precise,
Trenchant reference to their work,
And cunning questioning
Of their skill in wielding words.

Time now to exploit all manner of weakness.
Let all that is tired and uninspired
Be harshly spotlighted,
And let the enemy be seen for
Tiny, talentless lechers,
Whose words lie impotent before us.

Long Ago

How many years went by? I've changed.
I pined for you? Now, it seems strange.
My memories of you have dimmed,
reminding me of starlight beamed long ago
from far away in space,
a celestial sleight of hand. I know
that dazzling dot I see is a stand-in for a stone;
the star itself is long since gone.
Or, having fizzled out, it's dark, cold, and forlorn,
as if the marvel it was once, was never born.
I wonder now, *What was it all about?*
A lusty spark was lit and then went out.

Is there a soul somewhere preserved in cosmic dust?
Can I brush off the traces of this old love at last?

Venere Callipige (or *Aphrodite Kallipygos*)
Source: Museo archeologico nazionale di Napoli.
Collezione Farnese.

Epigram

Venus, I leave this modest tribute, if you will,
a thank you note,
the kind inscribed in temples or at the feet of statues
erected in honour of a god, some poet or Augustus,
casting his shadow still by way of statutes and codes,
as always, glorifying manliness.

Venus, goddess of love, sex, and fertility,
apogee of beauty and appeal, star among gods and
nymphs—
here is my obeisance: a hymn to your influence,
inimitable gifts to bards,
and parts you played in epic tales of passion, betrayal,
war, and greater forces ruling the destinies of mortals.

Doubtless, Apollo and Calliope deserve their dues.
It's customary, more or less.
Yet it was you, goddess, who set the wheels in motion in
Homer's sagas.
Virgil made you dame of Rome as mother to Aeneas.
Or didn't the Portuguese Camões attribute
Vasco da Gama's
successful voyages to you in *Os Lusíadas?*

Then may this earnest inscription serve as praise.
On the Parnassian hilltop, or, better, stage,
among exalted muses, you've earned the loftiest place.
No need for modesty. Lady, take your bow.
You've never been demure. Don't start pretending now.

An Hour Forward

Spring sprung us an hour forward,
Granting sixty more minutes in the light.
So on the one hand, it moves us onward
And at the same time, postpones the night.
This loss and gain in the rewinding,
I never fully understood;
I lost an hour, and now am writing,
Feeling more rushed than probably I should.
Scholars and poets are mindful of time's passing;
I, too, work and live by the clock.
An hour has been lost, and now I'm fussing,
Scribbling in double time to the tick-tock.
If you're a man trying to flag my attention,
Know that you'll never get your timing right—
I'm either winding up or winding down my labours;
My hours are always spoken for at night.

Reply to Mr. No Chance

His advice: "Slow down, let me sit back,
nip at the lines, phrasing, style." He says
(I imagine with a salutary smile),
"As is, it's well polished,
the wording—all studied picks,
'stead of being lightly plucked."
He prefers a languorous strum,
writing that feels as if it'd been done
with ease—unlaboured, breezy,
evocative of cranes cruising insouciant
against a gold and silver sky.
Below them—why,
a seashore's drawn-out susurration.
Above, blanched clouds nobly floating
in slow, procession-like thrums
of cotton, or frayed cloths
a coterie of laundresses
leisurely splayed out to dry
in gentle wafts of morning air.
He wants to be reminded of Tang Dynasty verse.
That could mean off-the-cuff, but deep;
light on the surface, dark beneath;
finely observed, emotive, albeit terse.

A sommelier, he can say 'yay' or 'nay',
(to my chagrin). He likes a tone that's leisurely, serene,
yet with an obvious lilt.
Poetry must *hummm*,
resonate with bluesy beat, he says.
This is a sine qua non for him.

Leaning into each line of an MS
    (sadly not mine,
        nor any Parnassian kind),
should be like savouring mulled wine.
Or is it that he wants to mull over each line?

His comments bring winter holidays to mind.
Festivities are over. Outside, a dog's bark
    briefly disturbs the hush of night.
He sits by a window. Snow falls in the dark,
    plying a veil of silvery white.
A wind barely ruffles the row of trees
    guarding his small property.
Beyond this edge, a creek quiescent lies.
    Orion's stars glimmer overhead,
signalling tidings from bygone times.

    He sips warmed wine, having read
a few of the lines with nodding head.
    It's late. He wants to go to bed.
Besides, the rhythm here—ho-hum;
    It's not that four beats per measure is humdrum,
but that the absence of syncopation
    doesn't jive with the absinthe in his libation.

I don't like the verse you write
The verse you write isn't all right.
It isn't right when verse is trite.

豉汁爆鸡球
左宗棠雞
薑扁牛肉
宮爆虾球
        (House of Chan)

How to Write Poems in Space

(for Joe F)

A much-admired poet advised me, *Go deep!*
Since then I've been churning away at these words,
wondering how to put them to alchemical use,
how to make poetry out of mundane stuff.
The question is:
Is it like sipping the thickest of broths through a straw
so that no particle passes untested?
Is it like sifting through clothes, years old, piled high,
each item fingered, each square probed
with straining eyes for stains or loose strands?
Is it like wading into the shallow parts of a sea,
with toes scraping the bottom,
every stone and shard made known to me?
Or is it like some form of folding,
the gaze turned outside-in,
seeing the scattered and clustered stars
and planets—near and distant—
of the blue-black cosmos therein?

In that vastness opened up to my inward eye,
I'd grab at the closest floating rock, holding fast
like de Saint-Exupéry's little prince,
my legs suspended behind me, lifted up,
space sucking my body without carrying me off.
I'd hold on to that planetary object,
itself kept in place by a string,
as if suspended from a ceiling unseen,
or moored to some distant shore.
I would float there,
in that silent place,
Forging poems
from the depths of space.

On Uses and Abuses
of Muses

Dear muse,
stay clear of artists.
Avoid the males'
oft-reiterated tales
of passion and need.
They are a bottomless pit.
They spit and spit
out muses by the dozen.
Dear muse,
sorry to disabuse
you of the notion
that as a muse
you'll be excused.
Be warned, all uses
an artist finds for you
are variations on abuses.
Avoid the poet in his den.
The muse is fodder for his pen.

Inspiration (or Philia)

Each curled grey strand atop your head—I bless
The crinkles at the corners of your eyes—I kiss
For all the springs you've seen as many more
for you—I wish
Stalwart and august, the formidable man—I see
Hearty and hale as you are now—I pray
You stay tall and sturdy as an oak—I hope
You live as fully as you have.
My handsome son, I hope in all the years
to come—I may
Keep close to you and share your strength—I ask
That I may lean on you at times—I vow
If ever it is you who calls on me—I'll come
Know that your causes, the wrongs
you want to right—I laud
All that distresses you or else
whatever brings delight—I'll try
To understand, protect, and, plainly, have your back.
I will respect the wisdom you've acquired—I'll learn
From you if you'll allow it—I'll show
My gratitude in countless ways, with kisses—I'll bestow
Tenderly on your dear brow—I'll bow
To wishes you express, and in all things—I'll manifest
My full devotion and the joy—I feel
Always, invariably, when you are near.

Ancestral Home

My mother's and my father's parents,
babushki, dedushki, cousins galore,
were born in Ukraine, in towns and cities,
whose names make up familial lore.
Odessa, Zhytomyr, Kyiv—known to me, places
comprise a timeline, lines of descent.
I trace them in half-remembered faces,
present to me like a familiar scent.
There are so many drops of blood,
or, if you will, strands of hereditary code,
that on an inborn, cellular level
Ukraine is a constant, an abode.
Ukraine, my ancestors' ancestral home—
bleak now, bleeding, another Somme.

March, 2022

Jouissance

I can say what **a poem** isn't. Like Socrates,
forever engaged in conversations, sifting or filtering
notions, removing common misunderstandings,
getting at the crux of the question.
There **is** no simple answer, but listeners are entitled to
a process of elimination. There is something to minor
terms. They enable minor insights.
This, in fact, is major—a truth **we can bring into play**,
perhaps joyfully, **when** moving the posts, reconfiguring
the field, re**considering the** problem of the goals of
poetry. Let us start with a qualitative analysis of my
findings, though keep in mind that I've drawn on my
subjective experience of writing, the *qualia* of my lived
anxiety
due to my *ex*-centric position
in this field, whose limits I'm trying not to transcend but
reform. I keep my eyes out for gatekeepers. We need
them, but, **generally** speaking, I dislike our current ones.
Still, I believe, and my data confirms this,
that we shouldn't try to leap over or ignore boundaries.
We should push back, especially **against** the body
of experts that is so firmly ensconced at the centre
and very heart of our nation's culture.
Why should they be making the rules, wielding authority
enough to say what a poem isn't?

Like Socrates, **I want** to posit that a poem is not
to be compared with a boisterous child tugging or
tapping incessantly, hemming and hawing her
impatience, **trying everything** to get attention.
Children say and do things **without rhyme or reason**.
Hence, we must watch and listen attentively.
They're not transparent, and they make statements

39

in defiance of **logic**. We know, **too**, that a series
of *non sequiturs* **doesn't add up to a poem.**
Let's agree: it's not what a poem does.

A poem is also not like a man bent on seduction,
who shows up at the door in a fine suit and Florsheims
polished, wherein his interest and intent are not to be
missed or easily parried. This man spouts **lines,**
half-understanding their meaning.
He's **imaginatively** hobbled.
This man—let's call him Dick—though **composed,**
is out of his element. He would **do better** in a bar than
being inauthentic and trying hard **to impress.**
His goal is to score, and one is tempted to give in
out of a perverse desire to see how far he'll get.
Yet this too isn't what we'd want if we were aiming for a
poem with staying power or even sex appeal—you
know, **something we** could show others without shame or
shyness. To put it otherwise, we mustn't be enticed
by any old pair of shiny shoes.

We **must** also not **consider a** poem as capital.
Not cultural, and much less symbolic, since
there is no **formal advantage** or benefit to be had
in a field jealously guarded by cognoscenti.
A poem won't put bread on the table, and it won't
make you friends (especially if it's good), so don't
view a poem as a source of social capital either.
A poem **isn't the kind of thing** that will please everyone.
Popularity won't guarantee quality.
Without taking the necessary steps, **a writer might**
as well enjoy her time in a pub, and not **labour over**
a poem **to hit some mark.** You ask, *What is the mark*?
The goal of a poem, for me, though I'm no authority
on forms or aims, **is to** experience and **provoke delight.**

Your Blues Become Me

Our room is shades of watercolor blue.
There's light and air, but no angels.
In our suburban sanctum,
when the blues come as murmurs,
we work on forgiving ourselves.
At times, the walls turn turbid, somber,
Muffling thought and speech.
The past seeps in like newly-spilled ink,
staining everything.
Then the room grows dense with memories.
We lie side by side, holding hands,
waiting for the grace of dawn, its palliating light.

Some days evoke nights at sea.
A doleful, heaving darkness
seizes our room, the street, the city's north end.
Our murky chamber
undoes tender gestures and glances,
and all the hurt you cling to
is weight enough to drown us both.
We bide the storm, watch for shifts in tone,
buoy ourselves on words,
promises of clear, crisp skies,
sightings of a luminous horizon.
We wait for the washed-out blues.

Some days, our room is light lapis
with curtains that fall like lashes,
where windows gaze on sand and sea.
Outside, white melds to green then ultramarine,
And an expanse of fluttering lights
stretches toward a gold band of sky and sea.
I see us back in Naples, on days like these,
walking along the speckled beach.
You laugh again, urge me to look
when spotting a pair of bottlenose dolphins
surface between the pillars of the long pier.

On days like these, the world is a vista of hula-ing lights.
And your blues are like the surf
stroking the shore, exhaling softly.
These are my favourite blues—deep, poetic.
These are your brilliant blues—royal, lofty.
But rest assured, I see beauty in all your blues.

Witch

Witch? I am—
No cliché in picture books,
hirsute, mean spirit, or benign
soothsayer of disquieting looks.
Not one of Macbeth's old hags,
forest-bound, cackling,
sneering at propriety, half-nude,
queer-looking and lewd.
I'm not a faerie—i.e., good witch
contained in a medieval court,
no wisewoman subtly enacting theory,
(thanks to BG) the fictionalized sort,
not one who transgresses—verbally or sexually—
some limit marked out by official rhetoric,
and then confesses under duress
to devilry, "the kiss" she didn't commit
(Holy Bejesus! Can we guess
how many times that came to pass?).

I'm no wild woman, witch in a ditch
of fiction (an inside joke) for folk
ruing innumerable constraints
related to gender and age.
A witch does with her body as she sees fit.
She gives herself council that's sage,
not caring one whit,
unheeding of the androcentric construct.
She determines her own course and conduct.

But perhaps I'm all of these
Women and more. Why not?
They were condemned for what?
For being odd, speaking
an inconvenient truth.
Why the order to gag and torment?
In sooth, what's there to conceal—
A head of hair, a shoulder or a leg,
A God-given flair for seeing true intent,
or a capacity to versify or heal?

So be it, I'm a witch—
that woman who'll
fiercely protect her own—
mad as a hatter, raging bull
who will, if pushed,
transform—be a bear mother,
fierce creature of any kind—
storming with every ounce
of maternal might, to smother,
thwart a threat to her child.
Or else, I'll labour over a pot,
adding herbs, stirring, stirring
in an apron stained through and through,
preparing a wholesome brew,
and willing, willing the cauldron to yield,
a delicious, sustaining meal,
brimming with goodness,
conjured with pure love and care
to nourish or cure
all who are offered this fare.

I Don't Love You Right Now

I don't love you right now,
though one day I may.
Right now, I don't love the you with angry eyes,
intense and beautiful.
(Pardon me for the unintended exoticizing,
and for nearly writing *exorcizing*, by mistake.)
I see you standing across the street
beneath an arched doorway with colourful stones
announcing the gateway to a home.
You remind me of a panther, with eyes that watch
and wait for me to lower my guard,
so you can spring and tear me to shreds.
I don't love this you.
You don't acknowledge the beauty in me/us.
One day, when you begin to love me back—
when you smile and called me sis or aunt or your Rita—
then I'll love and honour you,
perhaps more than myself.

January, 2024

Our Sisters in Iran

Why zip when you can zoom, beep when you can boom,
rant when roaring is an option? Why bend when you can
blare, or tiptoe around, or try to put out rage with quiet
words instead of taking action? A moldering edifice
needs bringing down. It won't suffice to frown, or honk
instead of howl, when lives are crumbling and cruel
injustice is thrown in people's faces.

Why turn a cheek? Speak, shout, kick! Don't simmer,
boil! Brawl, don't bleat. Do everything that hurt and
outrage call for. Don't whimper, be that gust of wind.
Knock power off its feet, and force it to rescind its life-
denying formulations. Don't yield. Defy intimidation.
Don't blindly follow dictates or bow to commination
uttered by self-appointed surrogates of Argos.

Throw words like sand into your watchers' eyes. Theirs
are not the eyes that matter. Ergo, it's better to breathe
in, grow large, and call out with a steady voice, than to
capitulate or waver. Their condemnation isn't worth a
hoot. Their argument with you is moot, since freedom is
sacred, and like breath is due to every man and woman.

Take steady breaths, then take your stand. Don't teeter or
bend, upend instead, and tear the rot up by its roots.
Don't run or rein back your frustration. Take arms
against tormentors. What's more, don't hide the beauty
of your locks. Blazon your worth, then burn each symbol
of oppression.

The Living

Is writing poetry barbaric now?
How is it that humans are herded from homes,
            shipped across borders?
        The dead are abundant,
                while hearses are scarce.
Abandoned in cellars and roadsides,
unearthed bloated in collapsed theatres and malls.
        Grief abounds,
                    flooding cities and towns in waves,
                    or seeping in like acrid grey vapour
                        into bunkers, makeshift beds.

There are no gods
        but grief is known,
                visible, felt—
                    like stones in the mouth and throat,
                    the eyes in mourning,
                    an ominous growth
                        fingered at the back of the neck.

Grief isn't metaphysical,
        nor quantifiable.
        It goes without saying,
            and can't be belied.
                There is proof in:
                    collapsed walls of schools, hospitals,
                        large black craters, the smell of

burning, stooped bodies,

    children bereft of fathers,
    and nightmares.

Grey-black shrouds of grief envelop towns.
    After fallen shells, missiles, and bombs,
the impersonal rippers do their grim,
    mass collections.
        These aren't the deeds of gods.
        Who needs gods?

Grief is man-made, like pestilence.
    Pathogenic agents are men,
        pressing buttons with numbed fingers,
      detached, eyes unseeing,
        like zombies.

Dying happens to the living,
    in real bedrooms, kitchens, basements, or
    sidewalks in green squares.
    Death is not elsewhere, in another realm.

There are no gods, yet the perps aren't human.
    Those who kill indiscriminately
        or rape girls and women
           are the undead, soulless,
    doomed to wander aimlessly
    in bleak nowhere-ness, in dead zones,
        of alcohol- or drug-induced stupors.

There are no gods. Myths are told by men.
  Still, in pivotal battles, there are the living
    with steel enough to counter a scourge,
    move others using words to instil courage,
      the promise of immortality.
  Even Achilles knew—
      undying glory could be won.
  It came down to strategy, faith, brawn,
    and grace that could be hewn from valour,
      not rank brutality.

July, 2022

Tennis Sonnet

The back and forth of tennis
is not like a restrained exchange
of voices subdued and
without a hint of menace,
but like quick-witted parleys
or stinging repartees,
with smashes, womps and whammies
served up by stroking nemeses.

There's barely controlled aggression
and calculating savoir-faire.
There's brutality for Love's sake,
heart-stomping, die-hard passion.
The brave can spar at such a match.
As for me, I'll stay to watch.

Tales

The Twentieth Century

Movement in the air, quiver of a small hand
glimpsed and heard.
Leo caught the playful shiver of a woman's laughter.
Delicate as a bubble or a note suspended, an instant after.
She was saying to a man in a grey coat,
Find me. Walk towards…
The rest was lost.
A meddlesome breeze covered her words.
The next moment, the woman in tailored navy
sped away.
An ordinary thing, it happened on an ordinary day.
The vroom of an engine waned, and Leo, without
knowing why, felt odd.
He paused, gazed on. The Ford convertible dwindled
to a red dot.
It brought to mind a flip-book simulation
of a motion picture.
The blot of red flickered inside a dusty cloud.
A tiny flame died out.

The sight of a woman neatly coiffed, departing,
Was like a pebble striking an unreflective pool.
It rippled the surface, dormant as a rule.
For years the layers beneath the tarnished silver
lay undisturbed—an analyst might say unsifted or
un-probed—until that day.
Strange, thought Leo, that the scene

would cause him agitation,
provoking images, sensations,
the residue of long ago,
to rise like flotsam from below.
Yet there, at the crosswalk, at an hour past noon,
he recalled his mother—the sun hat of maroon
with crimson flower,
her custom victory suit, a royal blue.
Hazy, this memory of her,
standing motionless and distant,
although he did recall an instant,
when she turned to him.
Her lips moved, words were uttered.
There was a gust of wind.
She held her hat down with a slender hand.
The crimson shuddered.

Leo stood among a throng of people at the port.
Some came to bid their family or friends farewell,
while others came for sport.
The S.S. America was a colossal ship.
Glinting in the sun like some storied leviathan,
it loomed over the crowded pier.
A gull flew circles above the upper tier,
emitting an abrasive squall.
Below, the sea lapped at the glistening hull.
Transfixed, distracted, Leo squinted from the glare,
holding his nanny's hand.
A red and blue flag billowed from the mast

above the deck where passengers had massed.
He saw his parents there.

A blast from a horn jarred Leo from his reverie.
The ship was setting sail. There would be a separation.
His father was being sent abroad to oversee an operation.
It was his duty to comply, he said, then added
in a self-approving way that
his posting came with a promotion.
Leo dutifully waved goodbye.
He knew he wasn't supposed to cry or show emotion.
His father had told him boys were warriors
in the making.
His mother, elegantly dressed, remote, was fading.
Then he remembered how
his dark-skinned nanny had drawn him close
to still his shaking.

Life Lessons

My mother was Queen in her home
This meant she didn't toil—not in the kitchen,
nor during meals. An accomplished musician,
she viewed certain tasks as beneath her.
She cultivated an air of cultivation,
attended poetry readings,
enjoyed her meals while being served.
Her husband sprang to his feet often,
bringing and taking away dishes.
My mother lorded over home and me.
I had to heed her wishes.
Whipping her hand across my face,
she taught me about oppression,
and to accept that someday
I would have a husband
with the same rights and expectations—
that I would cook, clean,
serve, and take away his dishes.

This was my training—
lessons in womanhood,
in what to aspire to,
and how to be good.
My husband's father was King in a home,
where his wife cooked, cleaned,
and looked after children.
The father sat back at the dinner table.

The mother hardly sat,
was often on her feet,
brought and took away dishes.
It wasn't abuse, but metrics—
The math of hierarchy, or
measure of uneven power,
bio-politics on the home front.
He was a mathematician.
He lorded over her, his home,
the television.

As luck would have it, the son I married
had also been well-trained
To think a wife should look after his needs,
Bear him children, cook, and serve.
Since I had an education,
the calculus was different,
but the hierarchy remained.
I had to clear the dishes.
He had expectations
that I would heed his wishes.

Oppression starts in the home, and
women are as culpable as men,
we read nowadays.
That may be true—although it's hard to tell
Who caused Sylvia Plath to take her life.
Some blamed her wayward poet husband,
who went AWOL.
She had to cook, clean,

and manage on her own.
With children to look after,
she trained herself to write at dawn.

Some blamed her imperious mother,
who was conventional and rigid.
She viewed domestication as a woman's lot.
Some blamed the other woman, Assia Wevill.
She took Plath's place, then shared her lot.
With all such tragic endings, who's to blame?
The world perhaps—mothers and fathers—
for promulgating poisonous logic,
and binaries that kill or maim.

Homes mustn't be for subjugation,
They're meant for love,
shelter, and consideration—
poetry, too, when time and ambition allow.

Moses ben Maimon and Ibn Rushd

Let's imagine that we are Maimonides and Averroes,
(may their legacies endure through the ages).
Somewhere in Andalusia, the scent of *Dama de noche*
drifts in through high, arched windows.
On a divan side by side,
we recline like intimates,
drinking *sharbat* in the flickering, dulcet dusk.
With our cups, perched on two octangular tables
inlaid with sparkling taluses,
we converse in Arabic, the tongue of sages,
finding such harmony and accord!

First, we discourse on the art of healing,
agreeing that every instance of creation
is the sacred handiwork of the Lord,
accordingly, deserving life-saving ministration.
Likewise with laws, derived from a hallowed scroll.
Eye to eye, in the glimmer of light granted us all,
we see that reason bends laws to reasonable ends.
Hence, to forfend blindness to Truth that transcends
narrow self-regard, perverse, cruel inhumanity,
we say in unison, let cogitation, charity, and empathy
be our guide, when jurisprudence is being shaped,
since—alas—each nation claims to abide
by commands the One lent all humanity,

while hoarding, with the other hand,
bards and their prophesy.

Night upon us now, candlelight fading,
in hushed tones and consonant notes,
on sublime sublimity we touch,
concurring that each of us can latch
onto a luminous fragment of the Most High,
by contemplating infinite time and space,
the shimmering heavens, the human race.
Such paragons of creation all espy.
Each is a sign and wondrous spark
of the fathomless *Allah-Elohim* above,
who lights our way out of the dark.
We say, *Adorn His work with all-embracing love!*

Phaenarete (Fainareti)

Phaenarete in Greek means "She who brings virtue
to light,"
the name given to an Athenian child,
born 500 years BCE.
Bringing into the light—ushering a soul from
darkness to light.
Ancient Greeks, classically patriarchal, kept their
women and girls at home,
out of public spaces, theatres, schools,
and off papyri used for writing histories
and philosophical tracts.
Scarcely anything written survives;
nary a reference or token speaks to us of once living,
flesh-and-blood women of the Athenian polis,
whether high-born or poor, slave, or foreign.
Bringing forth from the womb, the cave,
the state of unknowing.
This cavernous absence of female persons
(not of imagined ones, such as Euripides' vengeful
Medea) obscures the lives of real women in antiquity.
Yet Phaenarete's name traverses the
vast, silent darkness of bygone millennia
like a beam of light from a once-bright star.

Conducting a cherished soul toward birth
or aiding its ascent to enlightenment.
Phaenarete practiced pharmacy and obstetrics.

This is known because her son, the philosopher Socrates,
called her a strong, capable *maia*.
In more ways than one, Phaenarete is a figure who is
immortal in her own right.
A midwife, her sacred vocation—bound up with
generation—helped Socrates conceive
of his own mission as engendering virtue in others.
A poetic trope, her name also means "She who discloses
goodness."

Light and virtue are beneficial to body and soul.
Like any healer, her practice involved speaking
poetically.
Art made her words compelling, like those of a priestess
or prophetess.
Poetry moved the listener, steering even reluctant
patients toward compliance,
and was essential to the efficacy of any prescription.

Love Letter to Plato

(for Adrian)

Plato, Aristocles, which ever name you go by,
give this besotted devotee
a chance to speak—to say what's on her mind
and in her heart.
For you are her ideal man.
Yes, she knows that cannot be
if she's to take you seriously.

Yet you, Plato,
pitch-perfect poet,
the inspiration from above,
that inextinguishable light—
you are her true immortal love.
It is your form
she most admires,
is desirous of.

Oh, she apprehends
your brilliant machinations,
how you direct men's thoughts
away from foolish inclinations.
And she commends—since she aspires
to be true—your wily ways,
and so-called divinations
of what Love is.

It's Love that begets everlasting glory.
Those gory scenes of Homer's
are for the blind and weak of will.
No need to battle, cause blood to spill.
It's wisdom that grants might, helps men transcend
their limitations, and ascend,
with Love's assistance,
toward enlightenment.

Accept, dear Plato, gorgeous man,
this small but loving dedication,
a mere essay, I grant, at emulation
from one who is your truest fan.

Symposium

(Diotima's purported instructions and
invocations to Eros)

Instruct me Eros, so I may instruct others
Thank you for being here. Today we'll discuss a vital
philosophical construct—one that continues to shape our
conception of Love as a medium that transfigures those
said to be in love.

Speak to me, so I may feel your breath
I'll be instructing you in abstract and mystical notions.
As a conduit of sorts, I'll expedite access to knowledge
that's sacred—truths not gleaned from nearby sources
but obtained from spectral go-betweens.

*Eros, reveal yourself, so I may know you and not a
false spirit*
Your screens can remain on, but pay attention. This is
arcane wisdom concerning Love, its nature and purpose.
To begin, I'll disabuse you of common misconceptions
—those born of fanciful or facile thinking about the
substance of Love.

I pray, make me worthy of entering your temple
You were misled if you believe Love is a deity like
Aphrodite, be she the sensuous, dime-store type, or one
who is cool, regal—a Fifth Avenue goddess. Nor is Love
a slender youth bedizened in gleaming locks, who
bestows love like favours that call for genuflection.

Bless me, Eros, and may the higher gods bless you in turn

I have it on divine authority that Love or Eros (which is its proper name), should not be mistaken for a god; that would falsely assign grace, style, and general perfection to one who is — by definition — wanting, incomplete.

Grant me cunning and resolve, one that nothing will sway or dull

One's beloved is bound to be winsome (that is how Love renders its object). But Eros is not that. Though an immortal spirit, Eros is rough, scrappy, and dogged when pursuing a prize, or any object it aims to possess.

Make my love a love of true beauty

Eros is unrefined, but neither skittish nor brittle. It is crafty and resolute — not one to turn on a dime. It has a glad eye for outward beauty, yet knows its wellspring is virtue. It is drawn to both, seeing them as two sides of a shiny coin spied in an antique fount.

Let me desire the benisons to which you aspire

There is a backstory, which I'll impart: Eros is like one who has suffered privation and dreads it. Restless, ambitious, Eros is keen to remedy shortcomings. It strives for greatness in each of its aspects, wisdom included.

Make me covetous of all you deem holy
Eros is neither cad nor gambler, but possessive to a fault.
Besotted, Eros views the beloved as flawless and covets
them. Ask yourselves: which of us could fault Love for
desiring to make beauty incarnate its own?

***Turn my loving gaze upward, toward the beauty of
virtue***
Granted, Eros is an envoy of greater forces. Yet it is Eros
who conjures fervent desire—be it by prophecy or
incantation—so that a lover is roused and sees the
essence of beauty and goodness in a beloved.

Transform my desire into seed
Listen: Eros whispers of eternal delight with a beloved
and perpetuity gained through Love. Thus commanded,
by gods and nature, lovers are driven to dignify their
ardor, beget an emblem of their joy.

So that my love can bear fruit
There's yet more to Eros' mysterious force. Lovers are
made subject to longing, for one another and for the
offshoot of their union—birth that will nullify death.
Thus Love acts on mankind's yearning to transcend
nature's transience.

Thus will love be a means to eternal life
Love bears fruit, but the noblest are incorporeal—
progeny of potent intellects that thrive in Love's
embrace. Note: Eros' master stroke is aiding lovers 'give
birth' to works that win undying glory.

Bathe me in the light of the sacred

Love's handiwork is wrapped in mysteries. I confess that it is hard to fathom the dazzling, higher ones. My counsel is to lift your gaze and follow the lover who, transported by Eros, ascends and beholds radiant, unsurpassed beauty.

Let desire reveal the splendors of noble ends

Eros stokes a craving for knowledge, since lovers' souls fill with desiderata that mirror its own. Lovers reject carnal inducements, aspiring in time to commune with immaculate truths, whose celestial beauty they can transmute into apogees of invention.

Let noble ends lead me to deeds of everlasting glory

Temples are built to honour those who, transfigured by Love, surpass other mortals. Their triumphs resound across eons, like Solon's, whose prudent laws (blessings to Athens) refract the hallowing light of justice and virtue.

Grant me love that is pure and mellifluous as poetry

Know this: Eros rewards lovers with fame eternal when their works accord with reason, order, and formal beauty. Yet the most exalted are the poets, for their issue are like harmonies of the spheres. They give Love its euphonies of sempiternal notes.

The Mantineian or Diotima Speaks

All divination is poetic,
yet not all poetry is prophetic.
I have been labeled priestess, seer—
as if all wisdom requires a Sibyl
or ancient lore is hermeneutic.
I've been deferred to among men,
some busy expounding on a topic,
which clearly went beyond their ken.
Yet unaware, bent on propounding,
they kept on talking—intent, myopic.

You ask what question, which mystery,
provoked this passionate debate?
How was the central problem solved?
Why was my name invoked, and I involved?
To lift the veil (when all else failed), did I prognosticate?
No. But that's too cursory a reply.
I'll tell you this: It was a ploy, a sophist's play,
clever polyphony on display. The spiel—
of he-said-she-said—had nothing of mine.
(Read, indirect speech, each word and line).
I was misframed, paraded as a mystagogue.
I had my thoughts, beliefs, and words retold,
scripted (I grant) into a shapely dialogue
on Eros, Love's profundity—all
cast into a transcendental mold.

Truth be told, Eros *is* passion, an embrace,
A pure enfolding does take place.
But there's no spell that I discern, or godly act
to certify in my capacity as sage.
Love isn't a mystery to unveil or to vaticinate.
If I'm to adumbrate, drawing on learning
acquired by women over ages, then let me talk—
not as a prophesier, prattling on yearning,
unsanctioned augur, but as a poet, perceiving
Love's dual essence as boon and knack.

I'll gladly help unpack Eros, if I may cogitate
on Love—the ways it manifests, its forms of gravity,
surrender, and exertion, its countless labours of devotion.
There is no mystery. Yet those who dedicate
themselves to others attain Love's sanctity.
Love is an offering of faith, a promise made.
Love holds the infant at the breast, or else extends
a helping hand to aging parents or cherished friends.
Love is a burden and gift. It carves one's fate.
It lifts, transforms, as I attest.
                These are Love's blessed means and ends.

Villanelle for Sappho

Expressing desire in exquisite detail,
Sappho exalted feminine beauty.
Love is love, even in Braille.

In ancient Lesbos, in passionate detail,
She wrote of yearning in lyric verses,
Adapting the tropes of blind Homer's tales.

She implored Aphrodite in one manuscript
To quicken the object of her frustrated longing.
Isn't love love in any script?

Poets ancient and modern lowered their vail
To Sapphic lines of undisguised zeal,
Portraying desire in exquisite detail.

Found Sapphic fragments form solemn tales
Of clear-eyed desire and earnest devotion.
Love is love, even in Braille.

Fragments of Sappho live on in our verses,
Bestrewn attestations that love can't be deterred,
Lines voicing desire in exquisite detail.
Love's codes come in every script, including Braille.

Parabola/Parable —

Fixed dots, that's you and me,
lives intersecting on an axis.
The line of symmetry
sliced through straight
and burst the dome–
esticity we thought we made
connecting all the foci.

Not to belie the gravity,
it was the turning point —
a parabolic plot, let's say
perfect in its geometry,
this consummate mapping
of variables, graphing
the path of a failed relationship.

To visualize it, behold
our ground zero, this blasted dot
from which an arrow is drawn then shot
like a prayer said aloud or sung,
fooled by desire. Watch! Up the rung
it climbs, then stalls, arches, dives,
falls silently, and lies there till it flatlines.

What were the lines we crossed?
From which transgressions mightn't we recover?
What broken promises rendered us lost?
Were there confessions that no palaver
could smooth and reverse the course
of our doomed love?
Parables teach that hope isn't parametric calculation;
more like a dove released in faithful anticipation.

Poems in Parallel

Our story is a parable, an edifying tale, whose ending is pending.
There's no denying, love has us by our throats. It sells us a bill of
goods, stokes false hopes, and like a drug few can resist (try
telling folks they must desist from loving), it lifts, brings on a
high, then—holy smokes!—it tears away the veil. Chimeric love
is shorn of the lie. Now, what is left? A sad romance, flawed
formulations, stale declarations? It's theft!—this pathetic brew of
misconceptions, the slew of doubts we kept at bay, while the
foreboding grew, and bouts of worry mowed down the fabled
castles each of us built out of air.

We stare at skies, their clear, beguiling blues, thinking, *There lies
bliss! It's within reach! We've paid our dues*. At this point, Love
must release her mysteries, and shower us with coin, reward
with discernment, teach precious self-awareness, help us side-
step bleak, mournful endings, each spelling ineffable loss. Let's
pause. Love isn't a coin toss. Her trajectory can be ruthlessly
resolute. Sure, divine love misleads, gives no guarantee, leaves
lovers bereft, adrift, but, to be fair, only if they consent to it.
So what? Consider this! Who steers a ship when it is caught in
turbulent weather? Here's a new conceit.

Once, we were climbing vines, green tendrils converging,
diverging. Toward the light, we twined organically around each
other. We didn't rely on calculus or oaths. It was natural. We
didn't keep score, but sought out weightless space, light, a
modicum of solace from loving arms. All of it felt right.
Love burgeoned. We bloomed, by turns gave, took. When called
on, we propped, helped each other be, yet never mistook
freedom for license, were mindful of gravity, the dangers of
inertia, or unintended injury.

In life there are no givens. All pledges call for care and restraint.
Love stories ending on a sorrowful plaint tell of vows that
shouldn't have been uttered; they paint foolish lovers, snared by
an excess of emotions, made to lament their quixotic notions.
Love doesn't require blind veneration;
it thrives on loyalty, respect, and dedication.

Parapraxis

I confess, the phrase "Freudian slip" intrigues me. The everyday slippage it suggests, like clear ice beneath white snow, or white noise that signals a transition into another world—a blip in the force field, that's also a membrane between reality on one side and the film reel of another.

But more than that, the slip evokes a glide, smooth movement between depths of awareness—one surface level, the other crouching beneath wild ground cover of a gloomy forest, woods of Norse legend, where giant trees obscure the fading light with gnarled branches like wizards' arms.

Then too: the glide is a *glissando*, from one pitch to another. It's a musician's trick, this conjuring of sound, that swash or spill of water, or like a clarinet's *gliss* in Gershwin's *Rhapsody in Blue*, the sequence of notes charms snake-like, thrills, enthrals.

Glisser means to skate. A poet glides on lines, from one image to the next, then effortlessly reaches beyond, as if equipped with a psychic's receiver—to snare and rearrange our apperceptions without causing a tear in the continuum of our waking lives.

My musician father always dreamed of emigrating from Russia for the West. He saw himself luxuriating poolside, a sheik with nubile beauties all around, "like nymphs," he quipped. It was his reverie and vision of a 'conquered' West—Freudian, but not a slip so much as a fetish provoking an Oriental fantasy.

To plumb the unconscious, I'll take Woolf's vatic advice. She said that writing is like fishing at a stream. A writer clears her mind and waits. Then, once there's a tug, she reels in the line to find that she has caught a vital thought, disquieting image, or else something that's unanticipated, transcendent.

Initiation

I was initiated at the age of three.
Nightly, my mother read to me;
half-understood by me, the words
Made meaning of their own accord.

Pushkin made nightly visits to my room;
His verses told of love, hinted at doom.
I saw how love withstood all tests, including time.
We speak of this nowadays as being sublime.

Reading his poems, my mother's eyes welled up;
Her voice would break and she'd look up
To see if I had understood. Not always, still—
I felt an unfamiliar thrill.

One night she read a novel tale
Of Mary and an admirer, Gabriel—
The angel's thoughts and feelings were laid bare.
His love was one too ardent to foreswear.

Idolizing Mary with tender, aching words,
Gabriel confessed that he was defying his lord.
I listened, moved by love professed—though
Without grasping how Mary was blessed.

This striking scene was furbished by my mother,
One Jewish woman reading of another—

Ironic? Gabe exalts Mary's noble brow.
I saw no irony then. I fail to see it now.

Years later, in a Viennese school, I sat.
Mary came up while a pontificating hat
Belaboured the story of her chosen son
With whom Mary had been blessed—yes, that one!

Next spring, in Canada, not yet settled,
Mother and father, a little rattled,
Reached out to friends, and when able
Took me from home to home, table to table.

Once, on a wall I spied a cross. I told our host
I knew this story. I understood what caused
This wise, gentle man to die, and if he'd care,
It's an enthralling tale that I could share.

Clearly a nerve was touched by my retelling;
The Catholic listened, his eyes welling.
He nodded, smiled, but made no sound—
Poetry makes the world go round.

Mezzanotte

(for Mika)

Mezzanotte in Italian is "midnight",
An ending signalled with a word.
The *notte* turns into a coda
A *niente* follows—not a chord.

In German, one says *gute nacht*—
This ending strikes me as abrupt,
Not like the lilting *buona notte*
Lovingly uttered *sotto voce*.

It's a departure *con amore*
To say goodnight on such a *notte*
Or a prelude to *amoroso*
Or like the sigh that says, *fermata*.

Like pianissimo, but softer
Mezzanotte says, go rest,
teneramente, calmly, mia.
It's night—high time to get undressed.

Dear listeners, on this occasion
I wish to add a meta-note
A sort of *la riconoscenza*
For those I thought of as I wrote.

Forgive the length of this *poèma,*
I'm halfway there—*mezzo finito.*
Amico Marc, *grazie, lo apprezzo*
And the *Azzurri*—ditto, ditto!

Note, please, this is a playful foray
These aren't dirty words I'm using
But an expression of *amore*
That calls for some ingenious fusing.

I'm really hoping, *cara gente,*
And trying not to sound *pomposo;*
I love Italian, *veramente*
And *Italiani*, even more so.

I hope to strike *la nota precisa*
With this *poetico,* I test:
Will *Mezzanotte* softly call us
To put our anxious thoughts to rest?

We're now approaching the finale;
Di mezzo was three stanzas ago.
You're no doubt thinking, *finiamo,*
Life's short, we're hearing too much *largo.*

Friends, I'd like to end the ditty now
Tell you À *presto*, take my bow
And hope there'll be some quiet delight,
A dulcet note in your goodnight.

The Ovidian Factor

The poet Ovid has that special something;
Call it 'oomph' or the Wow Factor
No one could deny—not Milton or Shakespeare—
That the *Metamorphoses* was it.
Ovid has subtlety and wit.
And with a sly eye for foibles,
He seizes the all-too-human
In men and gods. The latter are more intemperate,
More prone to anger and spite.
But they make the rules, and change them
Depending on their moods.

So much disorder, Ovid implies,
Ironically detached, he scribbles on,
Not taking sides.
Ovid is the ultimate poet-*flâneur*,
Cool, unfazed witness
To passion and bloody endings.
He saw that beauty and innocence did no one any good,
(Later, Juvenal concurred:
Becoming looks provoked the worst
In those who thought them rivals.)
Pride and jealousy were convenient go-to's
When comely heads had to roll, like Orpheus'
And plaintive melodies
Were all that remained—well, granted,
Sometimes, reeds grew, or some lowly flower.
All were at the mercy of the gods,
Or those with power.

How chill is Ovid—always
Shrugging his shoulders.
When Acteon, a stag,
Was ripped to bits,
He indicates, *Ah well*,
The goddess Diana was distressed.
She was seen undressed, and
Since modesty and virtue are a must,
Ovid, in passing, drops,
Most thought it just.
Adonis, gored to death—*So it goes.*
That's what you get when you're careless,
And reject the warnings of a woman,
The goddess Aphrodite, no less.

Still, it must be said of Ovid
That he tempered tragedy—senseless loss,
With wondrous transformation.
Ovid's own hijinks ended with him in exile
And far from Rome, in remonstration
He wrote exilic verse.
Like Orpheus, dejected in his relegation,
But singing on, epistulating
That he, too, would not be silenced
And would delight all future generations,
Borne immortal, far above the stars,
Ovid predicted, and was proven right—
His light continues shining,
Cool but bright.

The Disappeared Poet

(For all those courageous enough to
stand up to tyranny)

He is believed to have been killed by nationalist forces
in the midst of the civil war in _____.
She was last seen being removed from her home,
accused of incitement against _____,
a regime without tolerance for truth.
So you know, I have become an obsessive collector
of scraps of news, grim signs, and omens,
as well as voluble declarations of support, and
Internet links that lead me to volatile places,
and murky politics where dissidents sink out of sight.

_____

I tell myself: A poet isn't a shadow,
a barely-there shimmer in the distance.
We hear the poet speak, and feel
a solid presence in the words we see,
even with eyes shut.
Confounded, I look for answers,
and picture a man or woman,
at a desk or by a window,
focused on a page or staring
into the distance. But there—
In that offshore refuge, this quiet gaze
materializes hopes and fears.

And though they utter truths,
such honest, private exposés,
is art, not reportage, we say.

The world has changed.
This is no cloak-and-dagger flick,
nor Cold War Havana, and poets
aren't malicious spooks to be hunted,
or, like Juan Gelman, the Argentine, callously banished.
Berlin has been made whole again,
Stalin's reign is over; although the night
of murdered poets haunts us
still, a poet can't be disappeared
without reverberations felt worldwide, you see.

In the West, where we think ourselves free,
we cannot fathom the sudden absence
or whiteout of disappearance, or imagine
erasure without a headline,
public disclosure, or open letter.
This isn't Fascist Spain, we repeat,
Recalling Lorca, and point out that
Chile's bogeyman is also dead, and
Victor Jara was avenged when, after all these years,
Pinochet's henchmen were convicted of murder.

We praise those with courage enough to speak—
Václav Havel, Nelson Mandela, among others.
But poets, you hear, don't aim
to don the vestments of party leaders.

Instead, they pick up the mantles of other poets.
The gentlest of visionaries,
poets are solitary people, and
the most unlikely crusaders.
Their words are lodestars
or salves that soothe bruised souls.

Nor can poets be made to disappear (know this!),
for their writing survives and will resurface
like ancient scripts that speak to future generations,
like beacons in the distance,
whose truths won't be dimmed or silenced
however brutally and blindly some may try.

———————

"This letter is a cry for attention, a cry to fellow humans,
including poets, all over the world, in Myanmar,
Colombia, Sri Lanka and everywhere that words have
been silenced, hearts stopped, brains bashed in. Why
poets? Poets without borders. Poets as witnesses. Poets
writing in the face of tyranny, saying *no*."

From an "S.O.S for Poets: An Open Letter"
(*Beltway Poetry Quarterly*, May 2021)

Helen: Takeaways from a War Zone

Helen blamed Aphrodite.
Yet she berated herself more,
realizing too late that by absconding with Paris
she had provoked a war, caused destruction,
subjected the Trojans and Greeks to loss and suffering.
Fallout from her affair with Paris
caused collateral damage of an unprecedented scale.
Helen saw clearly the part she had played in the
catastrophe.
She admonished the goddess for preordaining this
reckless love, declaring that she rued Aphrodite's
empyrean meddling:
Goddess, what other ruinous adventure am I to go on
next?
Would you have me sail to opulent Phyrgia or Maeonia.
Will I be seduced there by another of your darling
mortals?

This yields two takeaways pertaining to love:
First, passion won't be ignited
in the midst of economic constraints,
domestic chores, tediousness, and
daily struggles to earn a buck.
A getaway is required, a vacay, in today's parlance,
some exotic locale that offers great shopping,
vibrantly-dyed mantillas,
jewelry, inlaid with semiprecious stones,

abundant and reasonably priced
in that swish corner of the world,
and some transportable artifact
that'll hang unobtrusively in a den or grace a bookshelf,
enliven the place, *you know?*

A disposable income underpins desire,
as well as four-star restaurants,
described sumptuously,
with high-resolution photos of elaborate dishes.
Amorousness endures in the right context,
one that grants us a good night's rest,
and when on waking refreshed, we leave for work
without fear of daily battles with bigoted bosses,
or younger colleagues who'll say or do things
to undermine us just because—
for any number of reasons known only to them.
Helen didn't have to contend with such downers.
Of this she was conscious, and for this, grateful.

The peace of mind essential to a happy sex life
requires peace, stability, order. (Homer got this!)
It's often contingent on employers
who don't prioritize age over merit
or other bottom-line thinking
that excludes while purporting to include,
and, notwithstanding, presumes employees,
who depend on administrators' largesse—
a course directorship here, a TAship there—
will stay disciplined and silent

when their aspirations and life's work
are overlooked, neglected, dismissed.

What happens to natural urges
when institutions conspire
with sundry authorities (i.e., princes with fiefdoms)
to keep wages below the rate of inflation,
or cling to outdated dictums,
grinding down, subjugating,
making demands on workers' time
without fair compensation?
Might such conditions not smother desire—not just for
sex?
It's not like a jaunt to Santorini, Capri, or Ibiza, baby,
no matter how sensuously the scent of jasmine
drifts in through an open window.

Admittedly, conditions could be worse,
frightful and dangerous enough to extinguish
whatever iota of life-affirming passion remains.
One could, like Helen, find oneself in a war zone,
albeit, in the midst of a conflict started for no good
reason—not due to honour or sworn oaths to assist when
called upon.
Not to win back a wife, known the world over
as the most alluring of mortal women.
But for one simple, ill-considered reason:
Envy and spite; a pernicious craving
to balance one nation's failures by plundering another—

its pastures, orchards, lush valleys, citadels, port cities,
oils, and seeds of sunflower.

But I digress…

Here is the second takeaway from Helen's new self-
awareness,
her falling out of love when realizing
that neither Paris nor the lust he provoked
would do her or her loved ones any good.
Anyone tempted to fall in love should think twice.
Pushkin's Tatyana, to offer a case in point,
is too wise to fall head over heels
for the world-weary Eugene, despite the love he
professes.
Once married, she is exemplary in her temperance.
This levelheaded heroine proves
that a woman should think twice
before taking up with a man,
no matter how modish
he looks in his suit jacket (or tunic and cloak),
how heady his scent, and despite the poignancy
of his *billets-doux*.
Helen should have been more alert.
She should have known—pardon the cliché—
to look long and hard
that particular gift horse in the mouth.

Leonardo da Vinci's Mother

Ah, Francis and the priest are here
To ease my passing from this life.
Yet my thoughts are on you, *Signora*,
Since you eased my way into this life—
A full one, though I grant, not sinless
Ask him to forgive me, madre!
I picture you clearly, as if you were before me—
Your gaze, as ever, reflective.
If I were to paint you now, *carissima*,
I'd make your eyes deeper
To capture their cinnamon mirth
When teasingly I said your name,
Not Caterina, but that curious
Diminutive of the one you received
At birth from Jacob, your father—
May he be blessed by the almighty
Who granted life to all of us.

This beatific vision, *Santamaria!*
Your constant, tender regard for all my needs
And those of others is my great solace.
Catching me in *Nonno*'s courtyard in Vinci
You'd hug me to your breast—such softness,
And from there rising, the scent of peach.
My breath would catch
When I'd turn to gaze up at you,
Your umber tresses, their soft sweep,

A contrast to the rose-white—antique-white
To be precise—of an ovaline face.
Light seemed drawn to your cheeks,
Coral-tinged lips, fine mouth.
I grasped your uncommon beauty even then,
And father admired you.

How often did I paint you, *bellissima!*
I made so many versions
In my mind's eye and on canvas,
All those madonnas with plump infants—
All with your radiant love, innate grace,
And musing smile—reticent, serene.
Every virgin with child embodied your perfections.
The soulful suffering, forbearance, wisdom
I layered beneath your superlunary beauty.
And note, *Madre*, how you inspired the Oriental settings,
The natural wonders you spoke of, gazing past me,
I recreated them: mountain peaks, woods of thick oak,
Beech, chestnut, and the great sea
I rendered with azurite and ultramarine.

Your forebears lie in a distant land
Yet you remain my own, Circassian *donna*.
I declare, you were my salvation,
As I was yours, *spirito amato*.
Your rapt gaze, turned heavenward,
Brought me closer to God.

Venus chastening Cupid
by Giovanni Francesco Susini, Italian (late 19th century)
Image source: Met Museum

Excavating Torment
(Or Ekphrastic Intertextuality)

Have you seen an irate goddess strike her son?
Ponder the neo-classic gem, *Flagillifera Venus*,
wrought by Venetian sculptor, Giovanni Lascaris

(alias Pyrgoteles).[1]

Now lost, many admired the statue in its day.

Regarding it, aficionados of the plastic arts enthused,[2]
while poets paid effusive tributes in Latin verse.
Among them, Battista Guarini from Ferrara,
the city-state where art and cultured urbanity
hastened the Renaissance, gave his nod
in *Signum Veneris Cupidinem Verberantis*

(*Why is Venus Flogging Cupid*),[3] saying he thought
that Pyrgoteles's *Flagillifera* outmatched in craft
both the ancient Greek Apelles of Kos,[4]
whose storied paintings survived in muraled copies
of sultry Aphrodite rising on seashells from the sea,
and Praxiteles, famed carver of Knidos's Aphrodite;
this figure's life-like beauty earned her a temple
and faithful worship by Knidian citizenry.[5]

Exquisitely captured in her act of retribution,
the *Flagillifera Venus* prompted Guarini to quip
at the display of indignation: Why punish
the flitting imp,

and what compelled the sculptor to represent
such an impassioned response to Cupid's tricks?
Antonio Tebaldeo likewise panegyrized
Pyrgoteles's wrathful progenitrix (in emulation
of the approved Greco-Roman lyric type).[6]
Reflecting on her maker, he hypothesized
with this waggish observation in a hymn:
"I'd say, the sculptor vented his frustration.
He saw he didn't have the strength to fight
the boy [Cupid] who tormented him."[7]

This paean to an artist was penned centuries ago,
I note, while poring over time-honoured texts,
like some cloistered monk of old—ardent,
habitually hunched, absorbed in labours, mildly vexed.
Deep-dyed devotee of ekphrastic verse, I seek motifs
that animated poets over the course of time—
ones they transmitted with clever riffs
on Eros brought to book unsparingly.
I wonder, whose iconography did Pyrgoteles borrow
to render his arresting fantasy in marble?
Was his muse Satyrus's Grecian epigram
On Love Bound, limning the winged boy's sorrow,
for he'd been cast in chains, hands tied behind him,
to stop his wanton kindling of desire.[8]
Or was it Simonides's inspired plaudit,
alleging that fiery yearning and ire

drove Praxiteles, caused him to fashion
a comely youth, who boasts in spite of fetters:
"My darting glances alone give birth to passion."[9]
If Ancient Attic rumour is to be believed,
old Praxiteles, too, was in love's throes,
but chose to requite his suffering by giving
form to it, portraying the rascally amour
roundly censured for all to see and savour.[10]

Faithfully deciphering the stuff of art—
life, myths reprised, and piquant innuendos
churning fancy into tales of broken hearts—
I trace, in truth, countless variations
on Homer, or else this and that hoary homage
to scenes indelibly evoked by Virgil, Ovid, Horace—
here in verse, there in a painted image—
depicting humans and gods damaged
by Eros's heartless interventions.
I, too, curse the villain, but carry on,
hoping to glean how cupid came to be chastised
in Pyrgoteles's creation (btw, this oeuvre
became a model for other artists thereupon).

Huzzah! I'ved chanced on *Cupido Cruciatus*
(*Cupid Crucified*). Decimius Magnus Ausonius,
its author, was a Roman poet and *grammaticus*.[11]
Versed in Classics, he utilized the canon well!

Addressing his reader in a preamble, Ausonius asks,
"Pray, have you ever seen a painting on a wall
where Cupid is excoriated by women, all doomed by
Love?"
Next comes a scene, akin to one that Virgil fabulated:
A nether realm of gloom and lamentation meets the eye.
The River Styx courses fatalistically nearby,
while a myriad of afflicted souls, weeping, grieving,
mill aimlessly about this dark, forsaken scape.
That is, until bright Cupid suddenly alights
in their midst.
Having strayed in error into this place of ceaseless
mourning, he's disoriented, exposed.
At once he confronts an outpouring of anger so intense
that he's unable to evade or resist
these wrathful spirits of women who were ill-used
(abandoned, betrayed, abducted, variously abused).
Each relates a tragic fate, proclaims with phantom fist
waived at Jupiter, that Eros is entirely to blame
for her pitiable state.

Now, this unhinged throng seizes the fearful stripling,
and hangs him on a cross, calling for justice.
Here, Phaedra, Myrrha, and Procris
incite the crowd. There, Laodamia, Dido, and Caenis
advance grimacing with an array of ghostly instruments
to flay their captive, brandishing swords, rocks, torches.
Behold! Leading this frenzied host is Venus.

Still incensed and bitter, bristling from the humiliation
her affair had caused, the goddess demands satisfaction.
And though it's a cherished son she aims to flog,
she raises the wreath of thorny roses to strike the rogue.

* * *

At last and briefly, I offer this peroration.
Some see mischievous Eros as a representation
of life, happenstance, our natural inclinations.
Manifold forces to which mankind is subject
lend order to or else blight our relations.
But I say, Venus was right to flail her winsome son.
When Cupid interposes unbidden, isn't he to blame?
In her shoes, I'd have flinched but done the same.

Notes

Love and Death in the Multiverse
The many-worlds interpretation, one of the models of quantum physics, was introduced by Hugh Everett (1930 – 1982). Another notable proponent of this notion is the physicist David Deutsch (1953).

Witch
BG are the initials of feminist scholar Barbara Godard (1942 – May 16, 2010). I'm referencing the final chapter, "Women of Letters (Reprise)" by Godard in the anthology, *Collaboration in the Feminine: Writings on Women and Culture from Tessera*, which Godard edited. The specific section is titled "Derivations."
The kiss is a reference to the ritual of *osculum inflame*.

Prayers to gods
See Aristophanes' speech in Plato's *Symposium*, a Socratic dialogue by Plato (c. 385 – 370 BCE), where Aristophanes supplies a definition of love/Eros.
Aeiphanes (transliterated from the ancient Greek, meaning "ever-shining"), also known as the Pole Star, or North Star (Polaris), is part of the Ursa Minor constellation. Its Latinized name, *Alpha Ursae Minoris*, is anglicized as 'cynosure,' a word with its own poetic ring. Cynosure (from the Greek *kunosoura*, 'dog's tail,' also referring to 'Ursa Minor') now stands for "guiding principle" after the constellation's use in navigation.
The constellation Virgo has been known since antiquity. Each spring, Virgo becomes visible all night long.

I Don't love you right now

This poem references Mahmoud Darwish, a celebrated Palestinian poet (considered by many to be Palestine's national poet), who became the subject of a documentary. The film addresses Darwish's love for a Jewish woman, Tamar Ben-Ami, whom he calls Rita in his poem. The film is *Write Down, I Am an Arab* by filmmaker Ibtisam Mara'ana.

Phaenarete (Fainareti)

Maia means something like 'great mother'. It's the Greek word for midwife. The Roman physician Galen used *maia* as a synonym for doctor (*iatros*), a masculine noun, but applicable to both male and female doctors.

Phaenarete and her occupation appear in Plato's *Theaetetus* (149a-150a), which is a record of a conversation Socrates had with the then-young Greek mathematician, Theaetetus. The *Theaetetus* is a dialogue written by Plato in the early-middle fourth century BCE. It grapples with the nature of knowledge. In Benjamin Jowett's translation, the Introduction and Analysis section tells us that "in the *Theaetetus* [Socrates] has assigned to him by God the functions of a man-midwife, who delivers men of their thoughts....The attempt to discover the definition of knowledge is in accordance with the character of Socrates as he is described in the *Memorabilia*, asking, What is justice? What is temperance? and the like" (n.p.). The *Theaetetus* is widely considered one of the founding works of epistemology.

Symposium

This poem is based on Plato's dialogue, *The Symposium*.

The Mantineian or Diotima Speaks

Diotima is a character in Plato's *The Symposium*. Plato uses the figure of Diotima to explain the true nature of Eros. Despite being introduced as a priestess with insight into spiritual matters not available to ordinary Greeks, Diotima of Mantinea (the "mantis" in Mantinea may have been a deliberate strategy on Plato's part; 'mantic woman,' rather than *metic* woman, i.e., resident but non-citizen of Athens, suggests that she was a priestess/seeress) is decidedly a mouthpiece for Plato. In my poem Diotima, who might have been based on the real Athenian woman Aspasia, a widely admired hetaera (courtesan) who was exceptionally well educated and gifted in rhetoric, rejects her role in *The Symposium*.

Helen: Takeaways from a War Zone

Referenced here is Homer's *The Iliad*, Alexander Pushkin's *Eugene Onegin*, and *Discipline n.v.: A Lyric Dictionary* by Concetta Principe

Excavating Torment (Or Ekphrastic Intertextuality)

[1]Gian Giorgio Lascaris (ca. 1458 – 1531) was also known as Pyrgoteles. His works are mostly lost, with the exception of the *Madonna with Child* on the façade of the Church of Santa Maria dei Miracoli in Venice. The *Flagillifera Venus (Venus Chastising Cupid)* is mentioned in several texts, including epigrams composed by poets who were Pyrgoteles's contemporaries. Venus is angry because Cupid/Eros had caused her to be unfaithful with Mars, and to be discovered by her jealous husband Vulcan.

[2]Pomponio Gaurico (1482 – 1530) was a humanist. He references the *Flagillifera* in his book *De Sculptura* (1504).

[3]Giovanni Battista Guarini (1538 – 1612) was a poet and dramatist. He composed the poem in 1496. It was published in *Poema divo Herculi Ferrariensium duci dicatum*. The literary device of posing questions while contempating works of art goes back to ancient Greek epigrams. See the *Planudean Anthology*. To read another translation of Guarini's poem, the UCL Press website's publication: "3. Classicism and invention: Botticelli's mythologies in our time and their time" by Paul Holberton.

[4]The painter Apelles of Kos (352 – 308 BCE) famously painted Aphrodite rising out of the sea for Alexander the Great. Apelles was celebrated for the narrative realism of his paintings—so much so, that Horace is alleged to have said, *Ut pictura poesis* (As is painting so is poetry).

[5]Praxiteles (395 – 330 BCE) was born in Athens, and was known for sculpting the Aphrodite of Knidos (or Cnidus), the first life-sized representation of a nude female in Greek history. The statue referenced here was set up in the Temple of Aphrodite at Knidos. It is known to have been cherished by the Knidians.

[6]Anotionio Tebaldeo (1463–1537) was a poet and humanist. His epigram on Pyrgoteles's *Flagillifera Venus* was included in Angelo Colocci's *Epigrammatari*, a manuscript collection of ancient and contemporary epigrammatic poetry that Colocci assembeld in the 1530s. In the late 15th century, Italy went through a period of rediscovery, resulting in the circulation of

many manuscripts from antiquity. The first edition of the *Planudean Anthology was published in* 1494. Diletta Gamberini explans that at the time, it was the only known part of what is today the *Greek Anthology*. Colocci is recognized as a central figure of Roman cultural life in the early *Cinquecento*, a period of Italian art in the 16th century during which architecture, sculpture, and literature, including poetry, emulated rediscovered classical forms. See Gamberini.

[7]Tebaldeo's elegiac verse was modeled, like Guarini's, on various texts in the *Planudean Anthology* — this is to say, on ekphrastic epigrams representing the poetic style developed during Greek and Roman antiquity. My version is based on the translation that appears in Gamberini's essay:

> "She who strikes is Venus, Love is the one beaten, the creator Pyrgoteles; if you ask the reason [for the work], it was anger: indeed, the sculptor, unjustly tormented by Love (because he saw he was not equal to him [i.e., to Love] in strength), represented this punishment, because it befits a child, and because it is real." I would have told you these things, if you had not believed your eyes. (Gamberini 181; translated from *Epigrammatari*).

See also the UCL Press website's publication:

"3. Classicism and invention: Botticelli's mythologies in our time and their time." <https://ucldigitalpress.co.uk/ Book/Article/74/ 98/5520/>

[8]Satyrus of Callatis (3rd century BCE) was born in Greece, and became a distinguished peripatetic philosopher and historian. His epigram, "On a Statue of Love Bound," is dedicated to one of Praxiteles's sculptures of Eros, *The Eros of Parium* (4th century BCE), depicting Eros as a teenaged boy, or *Eros of*

Thespiae. Satyrus's epigram appears in *The Greek Anthology*, Book XVI (originally constituting the *Planudean Anthology*). It was translated into English by W. R. Paton as follows: "Who fettered you, the winged boy, who bound swift fire with chains? Who laid his hand on Love's burning quiver and made fast behind his back those hands swift to shoot, tying them to a sturdy pillar? Such things are but chill consolation for men. Did not, perchance, this prisoner himself enchain once the mind of the artist?" [§195] See the *Greek Anthology*. See also Tullius Geminus's two epigrams on the *Eros of Thespiae* in Book 6 of the *Greek Anthology* [§260], and Book XVI [§205]. In both, Geminus mentions Phryne, a hetaera (courtesan) celebrated for her beauty, whom Praxiteles was rumoured to have loved, and wonders about the effect of his obsession with Phryne on his art (see Footnote 9 and 10).

⁹This poem also praises Praxiteles's Eros, and is sometimes attributed to Simonides. However, it could not have been the poet and epigrammatist Simonides of Ceos (556–468 BCE). The latter died a half century before Praxiteles was born.

"The Eros of Praxiteles," again elegizing either the sculptor's *Eros of Parium* or the *Eros of Thespiae*, is an epigram also included in the *Planudean Anthology* (Book XVI of the *Greek Anthology*). Its translation follows: "Praxiteles perfectly portrayed that Love he suffered, taking the model from his own heart, giving me to Phryne in payment for myself. But I give birth to passion no longer by shooting arrows, but by darting glances" [§204].

[10]Telbadeo had quite deliberately framed Pergateles as the Praxiteles of his day. Gamberini writes in Footnote 13: "In several epigrams of the *Planudean Anthology*, Praxiteles is presented as a 'paradigm of the artist as lover'(Gamberini 185). Gamberini references Verity Platt's "Evasive Epiphanies in Ekphrastic Epigram." See Platt.

[11]Decimius Magnus Ausonius (310 AD - 395 AD) was a Roman poet, born in Burdigala, Aquitaine. He composed *Cupido Cruciatus* (*Cupido Crucified*) after returning from Aquitaine to Trevès somewhere between 380 and 383 A.D. The subject for *Cupid Crucified* was suggested by a wall-painting in the dining room of an acquaintance. The poem was addressed to his patron, Gratius. Hugh G. Evelyn White's translation of the poem's foreword is as follows: "Pray, have you ever seen a picture painted on a wall?" To be sure you have, and remember it. Well, at Trèves, in the dining-room of Zoilus, this picture is painted: Cupid is being nailed to the cross by certain love-lorn women..." (207). See Ausonius.

Works Cited

Allen, R. E. 1991. Plato: *The Symposium*. New Haven.

Ausonius, Decimus Magnus, et al. *Ausonius*. Trans. Evelyn-White, Hugh G. (Hugh Gerard). Heinemann, 1919.

Briggs, A. D. P. *Alexander Pushkin: Eugene Onegin*. Cambridge University Press, 2008. Fantham, Elaine. *Ovid's Metamorphoses*. Oxford University Press, 2004.

Gamberini, Diletta. "'Unjustly Tormented by Love': Eros as a Source of Artistic Inspiration in an Epigram for Gian Giorgio Lascaris, Alias Pyrgoteles." *Source (New York, N.Y.)*, vol. 41, no. 3, 2022, pp. 176–85.

Greek Anthology. Trans. Paton, W. R. Volume I, Books 1-6. Harvard University Press, 1916.

Greek Anthology: Book 16, *Epigrams of the Planudean Anthology*. Trans. Paton, W. R. Harvard University Press, 1916, 1918.

Holberton, Paul. Translation of Giovanni Battista Guarini's "*Signum Veneris Cupidinem Verberantis*" ("Why is Venus Flogging Cupid").

Homer. *The Iliad*. Translated by Robert Fagles, Introduction by Bernard Knox, Penguin Books, 1998.

Ovid, et al. *Ovid's Metamorphoses*. Johns Hopkins University Press, 2002.

Plato. *Theaetetus*. Trans. Benjamin Jowett. Project Gutenberg.

Plato., et al. *Symposium: The Benjamin Jowett Translation*. 1996 Modern Library edition., Modern Library, 1996.

Platt, Verity. "Evasive Epiphanies in Ekphrastic Epigram." *Ramus* 31.1–2 (2002): 33–50. Web.

Principe, Concetta. *Discipline n.v.: A Lyric Dictionary*. Palimpsest Press, 2023.

Pushkin, Aleksandr Sergeevich, and Charles Johnston. *Eugene Onegin*. [1st ed. reprinted] with minor revisions and an Introduction by John Bayley, Penguin, 1979.